9/11 UNVEILED

Enver Masud

THE WISDOM FUND

9/11 Unveiled
Copyright © 2008–2018 by Enver Masud

1st Edition
ISBN-10: 0-9700011-4-2
ISBN-13: 978-0-9700011-4-6

2nd Edition
ISBN-10: 0-9700011-5-0
ISBN-13: 978-0-9700011-5-3

E-Book
Version 12.07.10

Published by:
The Wisdom Fund
PO Box 2723
Arlington, VA 22202
USA

email: staff@twf.org
website: twf.org

Cover photo by Mark Oatney from Getty Images

To my mother and father
who instilled in me the values
I strive to live by.

"All truth passes through three stages.
First, it is ridiculed.
Second, it is violently opposed.
Third, it is accepted as self-evident."
—Arthur Schopenhauer
1788–1860

Preface

The book is intended primarily for persons who dismiss other explanations of 9/11 as "conspiracy theory".

By definition, all explanations of 9/11 are conspiracy theories. The issue is whether or not a particular theory is supported by the facts. The facts don't support the official "conspiracy theory".

Furthermore, those who dismiss other explanations of 9/11 as "conspiracy theory" undermine their position by refusing to face their critics in professional forums— the generally accepted venue where scientists and engineers present their views and respond to questions.

Purposely brief, *9/11 Unveiled* summarizes about eight years of research (10 to 20 hours per week) worth about one half million dollars. Supporting documents and exhibits may be viewed at The Wisdom Fund website.

This book would not have been possible without the effort of countless patriotic Americans who are working to uncover the truth about 9/11.

Enver Masud
2012

Links to sources, photos, videos
click on section titles
and/or go to
The Wisdom Fund
twf.org/911.html

Contents

"Military experts from previous administrations told Congress today that the $300 billion annual Pentagon budget could be safely cut in half over the next decade".
—*The Washington Post*, December 13, 1989

"Preserving the desirable strategic situation in which the United States now finds itself requires a globally preeminent military capability . . . the process of transformation . . . is likely to be a long one, absent some catastrophic and catalyzing event—like a new Pearl Harbor."
—*Rebuilding America's Defenses*,
The Project for the New American Century,
September 2000

Attack, Response

On September 11, 2001, America was attacked.

At 8:47 a.m., American Airlines Flight 11—a Boeing 767 out of Boston bound for Los Angeles, crashed into the north tower of the World Trade Center in New York.

At 9:03 a.m., United Airlines Flight 175—a Boeing 767 out of Boston bound for Los Angeles, crashed into the south tower.

At 9:38 a.m., American Airlines Flight 77—a Boeing 757 out of Washington's Dulles International Airport bound for Los Angeles, crashed into the western wall of the Pentagon.

At 10:03 a.m., United Airlines Flight 93—a Boeing 757 out of Newark bound for San Francisco, crashed near Pittsburgh.

The 110-story towers of the World Trade Center were obliterated. The Pentagon suffered massive damage. Aircraft debris was found in Pennsylvania.

According to reports, the death toll was 2750 persons—mostly civilian nationals of 90 countries—at the World Trade Center, 125 persons at the Pentagon, and 265 passengers and crew on the four planes.

Seven years later, what really happened on 9/11 remains shrouded in a veil of doubts and secrecy.

Terrorists were reported to have hijacked the planes. Two days later, Secretary of State Colin Powell identified Osama Bin Laden as the prime suspect.

Europol's director, Jurgen Storbeck, stated (*Telegraph*, September 15, 2001): "It's possible that he [bin Laden] was informed about the operation; it's even possible that he influenced it; but he's probably not the man who steered every action or controlled the detailed plan."

On September 16, President Bush, brushing off doubts about Osama bin Laden, declared a "crusade" to "rid the world of evil-doers".

On the day of the attack on America, the *Washington Times* quoted a paper by the Army School of Advanced Military Studies which said that the MOSSAD, the Israeli intelligence service, "Has capability to target U.S. forces and make it look like a Palestinian/Arab act."

After 9/11, dozens of Israelis were reported to have been arrested, but the role played by this "huge Israeli spy ring that may have trailed suspected al-Qaeda members in the United States without informing federal authorities" remained unclear, and "it is no longer tenable to dismiss the possibility of an Israeli angle in this story," wrote Justin Raimondo (antiwar.com, March 8, 2002).

Field reports by Drug Enforcement Administration agents, and other U.S. law enforcement officials, on the alleged Israeli spy ring have been compiled in a 60-page document (John F. Sugg, *Weekly Planet*, April 22, 2002).

> DEA agents say that the 60-page document was a draft intended as the base for a 250-page report. The larger report has not been produced because of the volatile nature of

suggesting that Israel spies on America's deepest secrets.

Others suggest that Israel's MOSSAD had fore-knowledge of 9/11. Fox News' Carl Cameron did a 4-part series on this episode (December 2001) .

The attacks on 9/11 led to the U.S. war on Afghanistan—a war planned prior to 9/11, after negotiations with the Taliban for a pipeline had broken down.

The Taliban, after initially negotiating with Unocal, had begun showing a preference for Bridas Corporation of Argentina. During the negotiations—which ocurred prior to 9/11—"U.S. representatives told the Taliban (Jean-Charles Brisard and Guillaume Dasquie, *Bin Laden, The Forbidden Truth*), 'either you accept our offer of a carpet of gold, or we bury you under a carpet of bombs'."

Niaz Naik, a former Pakistani Foreign Secretary, was told by senior American officials in mid-July that military action against Afghanistan would go ahead by the middle of October (BBC News, September 18, 2001).

And the *Irish Times* (February 11, 2002) reported:

> The Pakistani President, Gen. Pervez Musharraf, and the Afghan interim leader, Mr. Hamid Karzai, agreed yesterday that their two countries should develop "mutual brotherly relations and cooperate in all spheres of activity"— including a proposed gas pipeline from Central Asia to Pakistan via Afghanistan.

It is curious that these two leaders, who only later vowed to "bury the recent history of poisonous relations" between their nations (*Washington Post*, April 3, 2002), could agree so quickly to the pipeline. Afghanistan's interim president Hamid Karzai, and Zalmay Khalilzad, the Bush-appointed special envoy to Afghanistan, probably facilitated the agreement.

According to George Monbiot (*Guardian*, February 12):

> Both Hamid Karzai, the interim president, and Zalmay Khalilzad, the U.S. special envoy, were formerly employed as consultants to Unocal, the U.S. oil company which spent much of the 1990s seeking to build a pipeline through Afghanistan.

Zalmay Khalilzad drew up Unocal's risk analysis on its proposed trans-Afghan gas pipeline. In 2003, Zalmay Khalizad became the U.S. ambassador to Afghanistan, and on June 22, 2005 was sworn in as ambassador to Iraq.

While the identities of the hijackers remained in doubt, despite U.S. statements that 15 of the 19 alleged hijackers were citizens of Saudi Arabia, despite the fact that the Taliban had stated their willingness to give up Osama bin Laden for trial to an international court, on October 7, 2001, without the benefit of a UN resolution, the United States, Canada and the United Kingdom launched their war on Afghanistan—one of the world's poorest countries, already devastated by 23 years of war and civil strife resulting from the Russian invasion of 1979.

U.S. Ambassador John Negroponte said (Irwin Arieff, Reuters, October 8, 2001), in a letter to the

15-nation Security Council, that the investigation into the attacks on his country "has obtained clear and compelling information that the al-Qaeda organization, which is supported by the Taliban regime in Afghanistan, had a central role in the attacks."

The letter added, "there is still much we do not know. Our inquiry is in its early stages"—but that did not prevent the U.S. from launching a war on Afghanistan.

The attack on Afghanistan created a million new refugees (adding to the existing five or six million), caused the death of 5,000 civilians by bombing, another 20,000 were killed indirectly.

President George H. W. Bush is reported to have told U.S. troops in Kuwait that they were "doing the Lord's work" (AFP, January 19, 2000)—President George W. Bush claimed "he was told by God to invade Iraq and attack Osama bin Laden's stronghold of Afghanistan" (*Independent*, October 7, 2005).

More than six months after the U.S. launched its "war on terrorism," hard evidence regarding the 9/11 attack remained scarce.

FBI Director Robert S. Mueller III admitted (*Los Angeles Times*, April 30, 2002):

> In our investigation, we have not uncovered a single piece of paper—either here in the United States, or in the treasure trove of information that has turned up in Afghanistan and elsewhere—that mentioned any aspect of the September 11 plot.

The war on Afghanistan seemed to follow the script

written by The Project for the New American Century.

Award-winning journalist, author, and filmmaker, John Pilger, wrote (December 16, 2002):

> Two years ago a project set up by the men who now surround George W. Bush said what America needed was 'a new Pearl Harbor'. Its published aims have, alarmingly, come true.

Thousands of Muslim immigrants were rounded up after the attacks of September 11. They were subjected to long-term detentions without due process of law, and immediate deportation. The homes and offices of prominent Muslim leaders were raided. There was FBI surveillance of Muslim activity, secret evidence was used by government prosecutors, and several Islamic charities were closed.

Next it was Iraq's turn—the decision had been made in the immediate aftermath of 9/11 (Chalmers Johnson, *The Sorrows of Empire,* 2004):

> In the hours immediately following the September 11, 2001 attacks . . . Rumsfeld again insisted that Iraq should be "a principal target of the first round in the war against terrorism." The president allegedly replied that "public opinion has to be prepared before a move against Iraq is possible".

Prodded by the neocons, on March 19, 2003, the U.S. launched a preemptive war on Iraq.

Israeli journalist Ari Shavit (*Haaretz*, April 5, 2003) wrote:

> The war in Iraq was conceived by 25 neo-

conservative intellectuals, most of them Jewish, who are pushing President Bush to change the course of history.

In June 2005, Michael Smith, a reporter for the *Sunday Times* of London, revealed the secret Downing Street memo, dated July 23, 2002, outlining an agreement between President Bush and Prime Minister Tony Blair to fix the facts and intelligence on Iraq.

> Bush wanted to remove Saddam, through military action, justified by the conjunction of terrorism and WMD. But the intelligence and facts were being fixed around the policy.

To further prepare Americans for war, they were led to believe that Islamic extremists were responsible for anthrax attacks in the U.S. that began on September 18, 2001, and continued for several weeks.

White House officials repeatedly pressed FBI Director Robert Mueller to prove that the attacks were a second-wave assault by al-Qaeda (James Gordon Meeks, *New York Daily News*, August 2, 2008).

> On October 15, 2001, President Bush said, "There may be some possible link" to Bin Laden, adding, "I wouldn't put it past him." Vice President Cheney also said Bin Laden's henchmen were trained "how to deploy and use these kinds of substances, so you start to piece it all together."

> But by then the FBI already knew anthrax spilling out of letters addressed to media outlets and to a U.S. senator was a military strain of the bioweapon.

On October 18, 2001, Senator McCain, on the David Letterman show, said the anthrax may have come from Iraq, and that Iraq was the "second phase" of the war in Afghanistan.

Several days later, on *Meet the Press*, Joe Lieberman made a "concerted effort to try and link the anthrax in the public mind to Saddam Hussein" and to Iraq and Islamic radicalism (democracynow.org, August 4, 2008).

9/11 was a godsend for the U.S. military-industrial complex. A $48 billion increase in the defense budget sailed through both houses of Congress, bringing U.S. military spending to $379 billion.

This represented (*Washington Post,* January 27, 2002)

> the biggest one-year rise since the Reagan buildup two decades ago and a suspension of "the peace dividend." . . . It matches the combined military spending of the 15 countries with the next biggest defense budgets.

U.S. energy companies also received a dividend.

In July 2008, ExxonMobil, Shell, BP and Total were granted no-bid contracts in Iraq (Naomi Klein, democracynow.org, July 15, 2008)

> to manage existing fields in Iraq and hold onto 75 percent of the worth of those contracts and leave only 25 percent for Iraqis . . . where 51 percent for the country is the baseline for new exploration, for new fields.

In the past couple of years, many Americans have begun to believe that the U.S. government's version of 9/11 is either incomplete, or incorrect.

In August 2006, *Scripps Howard News Service* reported:

> More than a third of the American public suspects that federal officials assisted in the 9/11 terrorist attacks or took no action to stop them so the United States could go to war in the Middle East, according to a new Scripps Howard/Ohio University poll.

In September 2006, *Time* magazine reported that 36 percent of Americans believed the government's complicity in the events of 9/11.

In October 2006, *Angus Reid Global Monitor* reported:

> Many adults in the United States believe the current federal government has not been completely forthcoming on the issue of the 9/11 terrorist attacks, according to a poll by the New York Times and CBS News. 53 per cent of respondents think the Bush administration is hiding something, and 28 per cent believe it is lying.

The 9/11 Commission's chairman Thomas H. Kean and vice-chairman Lee H. Hamilton have written that they were "setup to fail" (*Without Precedent: The Inside Story of the 9/11 Commission*, 2007). Senator Max Cleland resigned from the 9/11 Commission saying "It's a scam". Senator Bob Kerrey "threatened to resign".

The 9/11 investigation was directed by Philip Zelikow who divided the staff into nine teams: al-Qaeda and its history, intelligence collection, counter-terrorism policy, terrorist financing, border security and immigration, the FBI and other domestic law enforcement agency, aviation and transportation security, emergency response, federal government's emergency response (Philip Shenon, *The Commission*, 2008, p86).

A proper investigation would first collect facts, postulate theories about what happened, determine which theory is best supported by the facts, then draw conclusions. This was not done.

Zelikow, author of *The National Security Strategy of the United States*—the new preemptive war doctrine of the Bush administration written for then NSC Director, Condoleezza Rice—had worked on the Bush transition team. He had a hidden agenda: connect al-Qaeda and Iraq (Shenon, p130).

The rationale for the war on Iraq, to eliminate weapons of mass destruction, soon unravelled, and gave a boost to the "9/11 Truth" movement.

The Family Steering Committee were the first to push for an investigation of 9/11. A milestone of sorts was C-Span's broadcast of Prof. David Ray Griffin's talk from Wisconsin in April 2005—arranged by Kevin Barrett, of the Muslim-Jewish-Christian Alliance for 9/11 Truth. Now Scholars for 9/11 Truth, Pilots for 9/11 Truth, Architects & Engineers for 9/11 Truth, and others demand a new investigation.

The demands for a new investigation are based on fatal flaws in *The 9/11 Commission Report.* The following sections reveal what did, or did not, happen on 9/11. But first . . .

Pretexts and Coverups

A brief review of pretexts, deceptions, and cover-ups may be useful in understanding how the Bush administration, the U.S. Congress, and a compliant media misled Americans, and got them to acquiesce in the wars on Iraq and Afghanistan.

Suez Canal

Britain and France had their plan for taking back the Suez Canal after it was nationalized by President Nasser of Egypt on July 26, 1956. "France secretly enlisted the help of Israel," writes James Bamford—former Investigative Producer for ABC's *World News Tonight* with Peter Jennings (*Body of Secrets: Anatomy of the Ultra-Secret National Security Agency from the Cold War Through the Dawn of a New Century*, 2001).

> The intrigue involved Israel launching a war against Egypt. Then, once Egypt began defending itself, England and France would go in as "peacekeepers." As part of the "peace," the canal would be taken from Egypt and kept by Britain and France. Israel would capture the Sinai from Egypt.

The plan was agreed to by Israeli Prime Minister David Ben-Gurion, defense minister Shimon Peres, armed forces chief Moshe Dayan, and Britain's Prime Minister Anthony Eden.

USS *Liberty*

While falsely blaming "enemies," the U.S. government, and America's "free press," have sacrificed Americans in order to cover-up for "friends."

On June 8, 1967, a U.S. Navy intelligence ship, the USS *Liberty*, was attacked in international waters by Israel's air and naval forces. (USS *Liberty* Memorial website—http://www.gtr5.com/).

> USS *Liberty* was identified as a US naval ship nine hours before the attack by Israeli reconnaissance aircraft and continuously tracked by Israeli radar and aircraft thereafter. Sailing in international waters at less than five knots, with no offensive armament, [the] ship was not a military threat to anyone.

Thirty four Americans were killed in the attack and another 174 were wounded.

For 40 years, survivors of the USS *Liberty* have been forbidden "to tell their story under oath to the American public." The cover-up of Israel's attack on the USS *Liberty*, begun under the Johnson administration, continues to this day.

What have successive U.S. administrations been covering up?

On the morning of June 8, the USS *Liberty*, sailing a few miles off El Arish in Israel, was secretly listening in on the Israelis who were then attacking Arab air bases from Damascus in Syria to Luxor in Egypt. The Israelis had occupied the Jordanian section of Jerusalem, and captured Sharm al-Sheikh.

And while the USS *Liberty* eavesdropped (Bamford, *Body of Secrets*):

> a scant dozen or so miles away, Israeli sol-
> diers were butchering civilians and bound
> prisoners by the hundreds, a fact that the
> entire Israeli army leadership knew about
> and condoned, according to the army's own
> historian. . . .
>
> At the time, Israel was loudly proclaim-
> ing—to the United States, to the United
> Nations, and to the world—that it was the
> victim of Egyptian aggression . . . Israel's
> commanders would not have wanted tape
> recordings of evidence of the slaughters to
> wind up on desks at the White House, the
> UN, or the Washington Post.

The pattern set in 1967—covering up for Israeli aggression, has been a major contributor to U.S. problems in the Middle East.

Cuba

Following the failed, Bay of Pigs invasion of Cuba on April 17, 1961, by 1,300 members of a CIA-supported counterrevolutionary Cuban exile force, the U.S. Joint Chiefs of Staff (JCS) drew up and approved plans for "launching a secret and bloody war of terrorism against their own country in order to trick the American public into supporting an ill-conceived war they intended to launch against Cuba."

Bamford writes:

> Codenamed Operation Northwoods, the
> plan . . . called for innocent people to be
> shot on American streets; for boats carry-
> ing refugees fleeing Cuba to be sunk on the
> high seas; for a wave of violent terrorism to
> be launched in Washington, D.C., Miami,
> and elsewhere. People would be framed
> for bombings they did not commit; planes
> would be hijacked. Using phony evidence,
> all of it would be blamed on Castro, thus
> giving Lemnitzer [Chairman JCS] and his
> cabal the excuse, as well as the public and
> international backing, they needed to launch
> their war.

Accidents, writes Bamford, were to be used to ad-
vance U.S. interests. Had the February 20, 1962 launch
of John Glenn—the first American to orbit the earth,
later a U.S. presidential candidate—not been success-
ful, the JCS were prepared to use John Glenn's possible
death as a pretext for war.

> The flight was to carry the banner of Ameri-
> ca's virtues of truth, freedom, and democracy
> into orbit high over the planet. But Lem-
> nitzer and his Chiefs had a different idea.
> They proposed to Lansdale [U.S. general
> in charge of Operation Mongoose—covert
> operations against Cuba] that, should the
> rocket explode and kill Glenn, "the objec-
> tive is to provide irrevocable proof that . .
> . the fault lies with the Communists et al
> Cuba [*sic*]." This would be accomplished,
> Lemnitzer continued, "by manufacturing

> various pieces of evidence which would
> prove electronic interference on the part of
> the Cubans."

In 1963, writes Bamford, the JCS proposed secret U.S. attacks on Jamaica and Trinidad-Tobago.

> Both were members of the British Com-
> monwealth; thus, by secretly attacking
> them and then falsely blaming Cuba, the
> United States could lure England into the
> war against Castro.

Vietnam

On August 5, 1964, President Johnson announced retaliatory attacks on Vietnamese targets alleging that the Democratic Republic of Vietnam had attacked two American destroyers on routine patrol in the Gulf of Tonkin—the USS *Maddox* and the USS *Turner Joy*.

The *Maddox* was in fact gathering intelligence for coordinated attacks on North Vietnam by the South Vietnamese navy and the Laotian air force (Fairness & Accuracy in Reporting, July 27, 1994).

In 2005, an NSA declassified report revealed that the USS *Maddox* first fired warning shots on the August 2 incident and that there may not have been any North Vietnamese boats at the August 4 incident (R. J. Hanyok, *Cryptologic Quarterly*, February 24, 1998).

In 1965, Lyndon Johnson commented: "For all I know, our Navy was shooting at whales out there."

The Viet Nam war led to 58,217 American deaths, and as many as two million Vietnamese casualties.

Diego Garcia

John Pilger's documentary, "Stealing a Nation," describes how in the 1960s, as Britain was dismantling its colonies, the U.S. conspired with Britain to receive secretly, gratis, and for 50 years, the Chagos Archipelago.

Between 1965 and 1973, to clear the largest island in the archipelago, Diego Garcia, for a listening post for the U.S. National Security Administration, every man, woman, and child was physically removed from the islands, and placed "bewildered and frightened," on the islands of Mauritius and Seychelles.

> At first, the islanders were tricked and in-timidated into leaving; those who had gone to Mauritius for urgent medical treatment were prevented from returning. As the Americans began to arrive and build the base, Sir Bruce Greatbatch, the governor of the Seychelles, who had been put in charge of the "sanitizing," ordered all the pet dogs on Diego Garcia to be killed. Almost 1,000 pets were rounded up and gassed, using the exhaust fumes from American military vehicles. . . .
>
> The islanders took this as a warning; and the remaining population were loaded on to ships, allowed to take only one suitcase.

Recently, David Vine revealed (*Foreign Policy in Focus*, April 3, 2008) that this

> huge U.S. air and naval base has been a ma-jor, if little known, launch pad for the wars in Iraq and Afghanistan. . . .The island has

also been part of the CIA's secret 'rendition' program for captured terrorist suspects.

Iraq

Dr. George Friedman, founder of Stratfor—dubbed by *Barron's* as "The Shadow CIA," wrote in *America's Secret War* that the United States "had supported the Shah's Iran in a war against Iraq in the 1970s," but after the Iranian revolution, "the Americans were looking for a lever to control Iran".

Friedman added:

> The Carter administration wanted to motivate Saddam to fight, but he had little to gain simply by fighting Iran. . . . He was . . . quietly assured by the United States that it would have no objection to his claiming his prize—Kuwait—once he defeated Iran.

In a July 25, 1990 meeting with U.S. ambassador April Glaspie, Saddam Hussein was informed, "We have no opinion on the Arab-Arab conflicts, like your border disagreement with Kuwait." Meanwhile, the U.S. encouraged Kuwait to continue its slant drilling into Iraqi oil fields. On August 2, 1990, Iraq invaded Kuwait.

A high point of the public relations campaign to justify war against Iraq, was the testimony of a Kuwaiti "refugee" before the Congressional Human Rights Caucus on October 15, 1990. She testified to Iraqi troops removing over 300 babies from incubators in Kuwait City hospital, and dumping babies on the floor to die.

On January 6, 1992, *Harper's Magazine*, revealed that the alleged "refugee" was Nayirah—the daughter of Saud al-Sabah, Kuwait's ambassador to the United States, and that Hill and Knowlton, a large public relations firm, had helped prepare her testimony, which she had rehearsed before video cameras in the firm's Washington office.

"When George H. W. Bush ordered American forces to the Persian Gulf," wrote Scott Peterson (*Christian Science Monitor*, September 6, 2002),

> part of the administration case was that an Iraqi juggernaut was also threatening to roll into Saudi Arabia.
>
> Citing top-secret satellite images, Pentagon officials estimated in mid-September that up to 250,000 Iraqi troops and 1,500 tanks stood on the border, threatening the key US oil supplier.
>
> But when the St. Petersburg Times in Florida acquired two commercial Soviet satellite images of the same area, taken at the same time, no Iraqi troops were visible near the Saudi border—just empty desert.

Scott Ritter, former UN Special Commission inspector, claims that Richard Butler, former chief UN weapons inspector, "deliberately planned UN inspections in 1998 to orchestrate a confrontation between Iraq and the UN so the United States could carry out its threats to bomb Iraq." Ritter makes the allegations in a documentary film, *In Shifting Sands . . . the Truth About UNSCOM and the Disarming of Iraq*, shown to journalists at the UN (Ronni Berke, CNN, July 19, 2001).

Eurasia

Former National Security Advisor to President Carter, Zbigniew Brzezinski, wrote (*The Grand Chessboard*, 1997):

> A power that dominates Eurasia [the territory east of Germany and Poland, stretching all the way through Russia and China to the Pacific Ocean—including the Middle East and most of the Indian subcontinent] would control two of the world's three most advanced and economically productive regions. A mere glance at the map also suggests that control over Eurasia would almost automatically entail Africa's subordination,
>
> . . . About 75 per cent of the world's people live in Eurasia, and most of the world's physical wealth is there as well, both in its enterprises and underneath its soil. Eurasia accounts for 60 per cent of the world's GNP and about three-fourths of the world's known energy resources.

The key to controlling Eurasia, says Brzezinski, is controlling the Central Asian Republics.

The "United States is pitted in this struggle against Russia, China, and Iran, all competing to dominate the Caspian region, its resources and pipeline routes" (Lutz Kleveman, *The New Great Game*, 2004).

President George W. Bush has frequently stated that the U.S. would leave Iraq if asked by Baghdad's leadership. But when Iraqi Prime Minister Nuri al-Maliki asked for a timetable for U.S. military withdrawal, the

Bush administration and the U.S. military leadership continued to pressure their client regime to accept the U.S. demand for long-term military bases in Iraq (Patrick Cockburn, *Independent*, June 6, 2008).

> The US is holding hostage some $50bn (£25bn) of Iraq's money in the Federal Reserve Bank of New York to pressure the Iraqi government into signing an agreement seen by many Iraqis as prolonging the US occupation indefinitely, . . .
>
> Iraqi officials say that, last year, they wanted to diversify their holdings out of the dollar, as it depreciated, into other assets, such as the euro, more likely to hold their value. This was vetoed by the US Treasury because American officials feared it would show lack of confidence in the dollar.

Sources in Iraq's parliament told Press TV (May 29, 2008) that Washington had offered three-million dollar bribes to lawmakers who sign the "framework accord" which will permit U.S. bases in Iraq after the UN mandate expires at the end of 2008.

Bin Laden

FBI: 'No hard evidence connecting Bin Laden to 9/11'

Bin Laden is the "prime suspect" in the September 11 attacks, said President Bush on September 17, 2001, and pledged to capture him "dead or alive."

Bin Laden, in a September 28, 2001 interview with the Pakistani newspaper *Ummat*, is reported to have said:

> I have already said that I am not involved in the 11 September attacks in the United States. As a Muslim, I try my best to avoid telling a lie. I had no knowledge of these attacks, nor do I consider the killing of innocent women, children and other humans as an appreciable act. Islam strictly forbids causing harm to innocent women, children and other people. Such a practice is forbidden even in the course of a battle.

Experts dismiss the video tape "discovered in a private home in Jalalabad, Afghanistan" which allegedly shows Bin Laden confessing to the September 11 attacks (NPR, September 13, 2001)—another lucky find, like the passports in the rubble of the World Trade Center, and at the Flight 93 "crash site."

In a December 20, 2001 broadcast by German TV channel *Das Erste* "two independent translators and an expert on oriental studies found the White House's translation not only to be inaccurate, but manipulative."

In a radio interview with Kevin Barrett, Prof. Bruce Lawrence, editor of *Messages to the World: The Statements of Osama bin Laden*, called the video "bogus."

Ten years after 9/11, the FBI's *Most Wanted Terrorists* web page makes no reference to Bin Laden being wanted for the September 11, 2001 attacks on the World Trade Center and the Pentagon.

The FBI states:

> Usama Bin Laden is wanted in connection with the August 7, 1998, bombings of the United States Embassies in Dar es Salaam, Tanzania, and Nairobi, Kenya. These attacks killed over 200 people. In addition, Bin Laden is a suspect in other terrorist attacks throughout the world.

When asked why there's no mention of 9/11 on the FBI's web page, Rex Tomb, the FBI's Chief of Investigative Publicity, is reported to have said, "The reason why 9/11 is not mentioned on Usama Bin Laden's Most Wanted page is because the FBI has no hard evidence connecting Bin Laden to 9/11."

In the months leading up to September 11, 2001, the Taliban "outlined various ways bin Laden could be dealt with. He could be turned over to the EU, killed by the Taliban, or made available as a target for Cruise missiles" (Alexander Cockburn and Jeffrey St. Clair, *CounterPunch*, November 1, 2004).

On September 20, 2001 the Taliban "offered to hand Osama bin Laden to a neutral Islamic country for trial if the US presented them with evidence" that he was responsible for the 9/11 attacks. The US rejected the offer (George Monbiot, *Guardian*, November 11 2003).

"The Bush administration said yesterday," reported the *Seattle Post-Intelligencer* (September 24, 2001), "that it would release evidence that Saudi fugitive Osama bin Laden masterminded the attacks" on 9/11.

> I am absolutely convinced that the al-Qaida network, which he heads, was responsible for this attack," Secretary of State Colin Powell said on NBC's *Meet the Press*.
>
> Powell said the government would "put before the world, the American people, a persuasive case that ... it is al-Qaida, led by Osama bin Laden, who has been responsible.

The Bush administration's case, Powell's case, has yet to be "put before the world".

On March 29, 2006, on *The Tony Snow Show*, Vice President Dick Cheney stated: "So we've never made the case, or argued the case, that somehow Osama Bin Laden was directly involved in 9/11. That evidence has never been forthcoming."

On September 11, 2001, several military exercises were taking place: Vigilant Guardian, Vigilant Warrior, Northern Guardian, Northern Vigilance. What role, if any, these played on 9/11 has not been explained.

The 'Hijackers'

Four "hijackers" are reported to be alive

On September 12, 2001 ABC News reported that "investigators have identified all the hijackers".

Among those identified was "Satam Suqami, a Saudi national on American Airlines Flight 11, whose passport was [miraculously] recovered in the rubble."

The next day, FBI Director Robert S. Mueller announced that the FBI had "identified most of the hijackers responsible". Mueller is reported to have said (CBS, *60 Minutes II,* September 10, 2003):

> A flight attendant on American Flight 11, Amy Sweeney, had the presence of mind to call her office as the plane was hijacked and give them the seat numbers of the hijackers.

Peter Finn and Charles Lane wrote that an attendant on Flight 11 used a cell phone (*Washington Post*, October 6, 2001), but six years later, the FBI admitted that two low-altitude calls from Flight 93 were the only cell phone calls made from all four of the 9/11 planes (Griffin, *Canadian*, October 8, 2007).

If an Airfone was used, billing records could provide confirmation of Sweeney's phone call.

On September 21, 2001, Nick Hopkins of the *Guardian* reported:

> After analysis of the passenger lists of the four hijacked flights and other immigration documents, investigators identified Salem Al-Hazmi and Abdulaziz Al-Omari as two of the terrorists.
>
> The real Salem Al-Hazmi, however, is alive and indignant in Saudi Arabia, and not one of the people who perished in the American Airlines flight that crashed on the Pentagon.

On September 23, 2001 BBC News reported that four of the hijack "suspects"—Waleed Al Shehri, Abdulaziz Al Omari, Saeed Alghamdi, and possibly Khalid Al Midhar were—alive, and Director Mueller acknowledged "that the identity of several of the suicide hijackers is in doubt."

The same day, David Harrison of the *Telegraph* reported:

> The men—all from Saudi Arabia—spoke of their shock at being mistakenly named by the FBI as suicide terrorists. None of the four was in the United States on September 11 and all are alive in their home country.

On September 17, 2001, the Associated Press published passenger lists for AA Flight 11, UA Flight 175, AA Flight 77, and UA Flight 93, based on information supplied by "family members, friends, co-workers and law enforcement"—the same list appears on CNN and the websites of several other news organizations.

There were no Arab names on these lists!

The "terrorist ringleader Mohamed Atta"—identified by a suitcase and will allegedly left behind at Boston airport (Peter Finn, *Washington Post*, October 6, 2001)—was not listed on the passenger list for American Airlines Flight 11.

Hani Hanjour's "name was not on the American Airlines manifest for the flight because he may not have had a ticket" according to the *Washington Post*. How then did he get on the flight?

The passenger lists published by the Associated Press, *USA Today*, and others note that these are, "Partial lists of passengers and crew killed in Tuesday's terrorist attacks, according to family members, friends, coworkers and local law enforcement."

"This is a very strange way to source such information," said Gerard Holmgren. He asks,

> Why not get it from American Airlines or the FBI? If neither of these were consulted, how did USAT know whose "family members, friends, co-workers" to go looking for? Or if AA and the FBI were the first source of inquiry, why a partial list from hearsay sources?

Gary North, an historian, also expressed concern:

> How did the airlines know how many people were on each of these flights? The airlines must have had a list for each flight. What possible reason could they have had for not releasing the full lists?

On April 19, 2002, Mueller said in speech at the

Commonwealth Club in San Francisco,

> In our investigation, we have not uncovered a single piece of paper—either here in the United States, or in the treasure trove of information that has turned up in Afghanistan and elsewhere—that mentioned any aspect of the September 11 plot.

In July of 2006, in connection with the trial of Zacarias Moussaoui—the "20th hijacker," the U.S. government published documents containing the names of the alleged hijackers, and aircraft layouts showing the seats occupied by the hijackers.

The 9/11 Commission Report, published July 22, 2004, left unresolved the discrepancies in the passenger lists.

Jerry Markon and Timothy Dwyer wrote (*Washington Post*, March 21, 2006):

> An FBI agent who interrogated Zacarias Moussaoui before Sept. 11, 2001, warned his supervisors more than 70 times that Moussaoui was a terrorist and spelled out his suspicions that the al-Qaeda operative was plotting to hijack an airplane, according to federal court testimony yesterday.

Lawyers for Moussaoui who pleaded guilty, and is the only person criminally charged by the U.S. with participating in 9/11, allege that the government knew more about the conspiracy than did the defendant (CNN, February 2, 2006).

One, Two World Trade Center

Aircraft collision and fire did not cause the towers to collapse

Two World Trade Center, the South Tower, collapsed at 9:59 a.m. One World Trade Center, the North Tower, collapsed at 10:28 a.m. At 10:03 a.m., CNN reported: "THIRD EXPLOSION SHATTERS WORLD TRADE CENTER IN NEW YORK". At 10:06 a.m., CNN reported: "THIRD EXPLOSION COLLAPSES WORLD TRADE CENTER IN NEW YORK".

According to U.S. government reports, aircraft impact would not have caused the Twin Towers to collapse.

The National Institute of Standards and Technology (NIST), the U.S. government agency responsible for analyzing the collapse of the Twin Towers, included a memo dated February 3, 1964 in Appendix A of their report *Baseline Structural Performance and Aircraft Impact Damage Analysis of the World Trade Center Towers* (April 26, 2006) that states:

> The buildings have been investigated and found to be safe in an assumed collision with a large jet airliner (Boeing 707 - DC 8) traveling at 600 miles per hour. Analysis indicates that such collision would result

only in local damage which would not cause collapse or substantial damage to the building and would not endanger the lives and safety of occupants not in the immediate area of impact.

The memo further states:

The structural analysis carried out by the firm of Worthington, Skilling, Helle & Jackson is the most complete and detailed of any ever made for any building structure.

Executive Summary, Table E-8 of the NIST report estimates aircraft impact speeds at 443 mph plus or minus 30 for AA 11 (WTC 1), and 542 mph plus or minus 24 for UAL 175 (WTC 2).

The Boeing 767s reported to have hit the North and South Towers were slightly heavier than a Boeing 707. Calculations show that they would have caused less damage than the Boeing 707 travelling at 600 mph in Worthington, Skilling, Helle & Jackson's structural analysis (Griffin, *Debunking 9/11 Debunking*, p146) .

Executive Summary, Finding 18 states: "the tower still had reserve capacity after losing a number of columns and floor segments due to aircraft impact."

Despite the preceding statements, in an August 30, 2006 Fact Sheet, NIST stated:

NIST concluded that the WTC towers collapsed because: (1) the impact of the planes severed and damaged support columns, dislodged fireproofing insulation coating the steel floor trusses and steel columns, and widely dispersed jet fuel over multiple floors;

and (2) the subsequent unusually large jet-fuel ignited multi-floor fires (which reached temperatures as high as 1,000 degrees Celsius) significantly weakened the floors and columns with dislodged fireproofing to the point where floors sagged and pulled inward on the perimeter columns. This led to the inward bowing of the perimeter columns and failure of the south face of WTC 1 and the east face of WTC 2, initiating the collapse of each of the towers."

NIST's evidence and conclusions are challenged by other experts, and NIST appears to concede to their criticism.

Thomas Eager, professor of materials engineering at MIT, who contributed to the official account of 9/11 says the impact of the airplanes would not have been significant.

Kevin Ryan, a division director who was terminated by Underwriters Laboratories for challenging the NIST analysis, wrote:

Of course, those of us who have actually followed NIST's investigation know that they could not produce any 'robust criteria' to establish that fireproofing was lost through forces of vibration. Instead, NIST performed a shotgun test to see if the fireproofing could have been lost through shearing forces.

The shotgun test not only failed to support NIST's predetermined conclusions, as was the case for all of their other physical tests, but it actually proved that the fire-proofing could not have been sheared off because too much energy would be needed.

The Twin Towers had 240 perimeter columns, and 47 massive, box columns in the core. NIST's damage assessment follows (*Debunking 9/11 Debunking*, p146):

North Tower: 35 exterior columns severed, 2 heavily damaged; 6 core columns severed, 3 heavily damaged; 43 of 47 core columns stripped of insulation on one or more floors.

South Tower: 33 exterior columns severed, 1 heavily damaged; 10 core columns severed, 1 heavily damaged; 39 of 47 core columns stripped of insulation on one or more floors.

Engineering News-Record explained in 1964:

one could cut away all the first story columns on one side of the building, and part way from the corners of the perpendicular sides, and the building could still withstand design live loads, and a 100 mph wind force from any direction.

To make the Commission's theory appear plausible, *The 9/11 Commission Report* claims (p541), falsely, that the core of the towers "was a hollow steel shaft."

In response to an April 12, 2007 "Request for Correction," NIST's Catherine S. Fletcher, Chief, Management and Organization Division, appears to concede—at least partially—to the critics.

In her letter dated September 27, 2007, she states: NIST Computer Simulations: NIST has used an extensive database of photographic and video evidence to validate the models used to analyze the behavior of the towers up to the point of initiation of collapse. . . .

The WTC Steel Temperature: While NIST did not find evidence that any of the recovered core columns experienced temperatures in excess of 250° C, it is not possible to extrapolate from such a small sample size to state that none of the core columns on the fire affected floors reached temperatures in excess of 250° C. . . .

The Goal of the WTC Report and Its Overall Analysis: NIST has stated that it did not analyze the collapse of the towers. NIST carried its analysis to the point where the buildings reached global instability. . . . we were unable to provide a full explanation of the total collapse.

NIST's analysis ends with the "initiation of collapse." NIST admits that "it did not analyze the collapse of the towers."

In room fires (Dr. Vytenis Babrauskas, 2006)

the maximum value which is fairly regularly found . . . turns out to be around 1200°C, although a typical post-flashover room fire will more commonly be 900~1000°C. The time-temperature curve for the standard fire endurance test, ASTM E 119 goes up to 1260°C, but this is reached only in 8 hr.

NIST also admits that physical evidence does not support their conclusion of fire temperatures as high as

1,000 degrees Celsius. In the samples taken from the site, there's no evidence that any core column experienced temperatures in excess of 250° C.

Since steel loses 50% strength at 650° C, and melts at 1500° C, if one were to assume—for the sake of argument only—that the fire was large enough, the fire was neither hot enough, nor long-lasting enough (major fires lasted less than15 minutes), to significantly weaken the towers

Richard Gage, founder of Architects and Engineers for 9/11 Truth—with 1000-plus members, makes the following points regarding the NIST report:

> The destruction occurred with rapid onset, at virtually free-fall speed, and with radial symmetry.
>
> One hundred eighteen first responders described hearing, seeing and feeling explosions and seeing flashes of light at the onset of destruction.
>
> The concrete floors were almost completely pulverized into dust and gravel.
>
> The structural steel framework was largely dismembered into shippable lengths. Much of it was hurled outside the Twin Towers' perimeters, some as far as 500 feet away.
>
> Tons of molten metal were seen by FDNY and others, and was described as "flowing like lava" for weeks after 9/11, yet its existence was denied by NIST.
>
> Proven chemical evidence of thermate, an incendiary material which produces

molten iron as its by-product, found on the columns and beams, previously molten metal, and iron-rich micro-spheres in the dust by Dr. Steven Jones (and corroborated by the U.S. Geological Survey, but never explained).

"These features are characteristic of controlled demolitions, and not office or jet fuel fires", writes Gage.

And explosions were reported on television news.

MSNBC Reporter: At 10:30 I tried to leave the building, but as soon as I got outside, I saw the second explosion, an another rumble, and more dust. I ran inside the building . . . and then a fire marshall came in and said we had to leave because if there was a third explosion this building might not last.

Firefighter on CBS Channel 2: We never got that close to the building. The explosion blew, and it knocked everybody over.

Fox News Reporter: The FBI is here as you can see . . . they were taking photographs and securing this area just prior to that huge explosion that we all heard and felt.

NBC Reporter: Most of the victims so far were outside the blownup building.

Witness on NBC: It sounded like gunfire—bang, bang, bang, bang. Then all of a sudden three big explosions.

Among those who testified to explosions at the 9/11 Commission hearings was William Rodriguez, "honored by the White House" for his rescue efforts.

Since the fires were neither hot enough, large

enough, nor long-lasting enough to have caused the collapse, there had to have been another source of energy to cause collapse.

Leslie Robertson, structural engineer responsible for the design of the World Trade Center, is reported to have said at the National Conference of Structural Engineers on October 5, 2001: "As of 21 days after the attack, the fires were still burning, and molten steel was still running."

In their investigation, both the 9/11 Commission and NIST, ignored testimony and evidence not consistent with their collapse theory.

NIST says (FAQ, August 30, 2006):

> The condition of the steel in the wreckage of the WTC towers (i.e., whether it was in a molten state or not) was irrelevant to the investigation of the collapse since it does not provide any conclusive information on the condition of the steel when the WTC towers were standing.

The molten steel may not provide "any conclusive information on the condition of the steel when the WTC towers were standing", but it is very relevant to the evaluation of hypotheses of why the towers collapsed. The steel at the bottom of the debris pile did not spontaneously get hot and melt after collapse.

NIST did not evaluate the use of explosives.

NIST rejects the "pancake theory" for the collapse (August 30, 2006 Fact Sheet).

In September 2006, Mete Sozen and Christoph M. Hoffmann, professors at Purdue University, claimed to have an answer.

Sozen and Hoffman concluded that

> the weight of the fuel acted like a flash flood of flaming liquid, knocking out essential structural columns within the building and removing fireproofing insulation from other support structures.

These researchers simulated the "top 20 stories" for "3/4 seconds real-time". Their simulation, like NIST's, says nothing about the collapse itself—it stops at the initiation of collapse.

By extrapolation, a simulation of the 102 real-time minutes from impact to collapse—which would have to make many arguable assumptions—could take 652,800 hours or about 75 years.

Other than controlled demolition, there is no explanation for the sudden, symmetric collapse of the WTC towers, and for the collapse of the floors below the point of impact.

Even though the "criminal code requires that crime scene evidence be kept for forensic analysis. FEMA had steel recovered from the building rubble destroyed or shipped" to India and China before it could be examined for traces of explosives (sourcewatch.org).

A paper by Niels H. Harrit, et al (*The Open Chemical Physics Journal*, vol 2, 2009) confirmed the presence of thermitic material in dust samples from the World Trade Center.

7 World Trade Center

The 9/11 Commission Report does not mention the collapse of this 47-story tower

On September 11, 2001, around 5:20 p.m., 47-story Building 7 of the World Trade Center (WTC 7) collapsed in about seven seconds.

7 World Trade Center was not struck by plane, its collapse is not mentioned in *The 9/11 Commision Report*, and few know that it even existed.

The World Trade Center consisted of seven buildings: the Twin Towers and Buildings 3, 4, 5, and 6 taking up the equivalent of about nine city blocks, and across the street—North of the Twin Towers—Building 7.

Buildings 3, 4, 5 and 6 sustained much greater damage than Building 7. They collapsed, but not suddenly and symetrically like the Twin Towers, and Building 7.

The 9/11 Commission Report tells us that the Mayor's Office of Emergency Management was located on the 23rd floor of WTC 7, and at 8:48 a.m. the Emergency Operations Center was activated, but it fails to mention the collapse of WTC 7.

Major news media remained silent about this glaring omission for about seven years.

Videos of the collapse of the 47-story WTC 7—which would have been the tallest building in most countries and U.S. states—while readily available on alternative news sites, have generally not been shown to the public after September 11 by major news media.

The collapse of the 9-story Murrah Federal Building in downtown Oklahoma City on April 19, 1995 was repeatedly shown on television, and initially blamed on Muslim terrorists.

Dr. Steven E. Jones, a physics professor at Brigham Young University, writes: "The specifics of the fires in WTC 7 and how they caused the building to collapse ["official theory"] remain unknown at this time."

Prof. Jones attempted to make his point on MS-NBC's *The Situation* with Tucker Carlson on November 15, 2005, but was prevented from doing so.

CNN's Aaron Brown and BBC's Jane Standley reported that Building 7 "has collapsed or is collapsing" before it collapsed—the picture in the BBC television broadcast is time stamped 21:54 London time which is 16:54 or 4:54 PM EST.

Diane Sawyer, an award-winning investigative journalist, interviewed a firefighter on ABC News Live who said: "At Building 7 there was no fire there whatsoever, there was one truck putting water on the building, but it collapsed completely."

Some claim that "diesel fuel stored in the building somehow caught fire, and created a towering inferno." But a report from FEMA (*World Trade Center Building Performance Study*, May 2002) states that this scenario had "only a low probability of occurrence."

Dan Rather, then managing editor of the *CBS Evening News* and its anchor, while reporting on the collapse of Building 7, said:

> For the third time today, it's reminiscent of those pictures we've all seen too much on television before. A building was deliberately destroyed by well placed dynamite to knock it down.

Indira Singh, a first responder on September 11, said during an appearance on KPFA that by "noon or one o'clock", the Fire Department was telling them that they had to move the triage site because "we're going to have to bring it down."

Larry Silverstein, the WTC leaseholder who stood to profit from the collapse of the WTC (Greg Levine, *Forbes*, December 6, 2004), was shown on PBS saying:

> I remember getting a call from the ER, Fire Department Commander, telling me that they were not sure they were gonna be able to contain the fire, and I said, "We've had such terrible loss of life, maybe the smartest thing to do is pull it." And they made the decision to pull and we watched the building collapse.

If Building 7 was "pulled"—a demolition term, when were the explosives planted? This would have had to be done several weeks before 9/11—it takes that long to place and wire the explosives.

Who had access to the building for a period long enough to plant explosives while bypassing the building's security?

Securacom, now Stratesec, was in charge of security for the World Trade Center. During the time that a new security system was being installed, the president's brother, Marvin Bush, was a director of Securacom.

The collapse of Building 7 is unprecedented.

No steel-frame, high-rise building has collapsed from fire, either before September 11, 2001 or after September 11, 2001.

On February 23, 1991, a 38-story tower in Philadelphia burned for 18 hours; on October 17, 2004, a 56-story tower in Caracas burned for 17 hours; on February 12, 2005, a 32-story tower in Madrid burned for 24 hours; on February 19, 2009, Beijing's newest skyscraper burned for 6 hours.

None of these collapsed like World Trade Center buildings 1, 2, and 7. Why then should we believe that on September 11, 2001, three steel-framed, high-rise buildings collapsed from fire?

Following the inconclusive, FEMA investigation of May 2002, the "free press" ignored the issue.

On August 21, 2008, Shyam Sunder, lead investigator at NIST, presented NIST's findings at a press briefing. A draft *Final Report on the Collapse of World Trade Center Building 7* was made available on the Internet later in the day.

"Video and photographic evidence combined with detailed computer simulations show that neither explosives nor fuel oil fires played a role in the collapse of WTC 7," Sunder said.

NIST claims that the collapse was due to "some structural damage to the southwest perimeter" by falling debris, and to "ordinary building content fires" on floors 7 through 9, and 11 through 13. This caused "buckling of a critical interior column", followed by "progressive collapse".

Engineers routinely design structures to withstand expansion of steel members. Sunder did not explain why similar building fires, either before 9/11 or after 9/11, did not cause buildings to collapse like Building 7.

The photographic evidence regarding fires is helpful, and it does show some damage to WTC 7. However, NIST admits:

> Although the visual evidence for WTC 7 was not nearly as rich as for WTC 1 and WTC 2, the fire simulation did exploit as much as possible the few photographs showing the location of severe fire activity in WTC 7 at various time during the afternoon of September 11, 2001.

Computer simulation, without satisfactory validation of the model, proves nothing—those sumo wrestlers transforming into an airplane taking off, in the United Airlines commercial broadcast during the Beijing Olymics, were computer simulations.

Model validation—a crucial step in the modeling process—requires that "inferences made in establishing the model are checked by observing if the model behaves as expected" (*Simulation and Modeling*, Prentice Hall, 1969).

In the NIST reports we were unable to find NIST's model validation criteria, the results of model validation tests, and discussion of other instances where the models used by NIST (LS-DYNA—"a general purpose transient dynamic finite element program"—developed by Livermore Software Technology Corp, and ANSYS), had been successfully applied to similar problems, or how the NIST model behaved with other disturbances.

NIST writes that "damage criteria required adjustment to obtain the appropriate strength and ductility of the structures" (p542), and damage estimated by ANSYS "was input to the LS-DYNA model as the final step before analyzing the structural response" (p565).

Simply put, NIST adjusted model inputs to obtain the desired outputs.

Others dispute Sunder's claim that explosives played no role, and videos appear to show explosions. Buildings that have collapsed without explosives do not come straight down on their own footprint. Forensic evidence from the structural steel is necessary to rule out the use of explosives in WTC 7.

Absent satisfactory answers to these issues, one cannot have confidence in the NIST computer simulation.

Architects & Engineers for 9/11 Truth argue that NIST does not address why the collapse exhibits none of the characteristics of destruction by fire, such as slow onset with large visible deformations that would cause the building to fall to the side most damaged by fire.

NIST also does not address why the collapse does exhibit all the characteristics of a classic controlled demolition with explosives such as rapid onset of collapse, sounds of explosions at ground floor a full second prior to collapse, symmetrical collapse through the path of greatest resistance at nearly free-fall speed with the steel skeleton broken up for shipment, massive volume of expanding pyroclastic dust clouds, tons of molten metal found by Controlled Demolition, Inc., the chemical signature of thermate (a high tech incendiary) found in slag, solidified molten metal, and dust samples by Prof. Jones, and rapid oxidation and intergranular melting on structural steel samples examined by FEMA.

Indeed, videos show windows being blown out from the bottom toward the top of WTC7 just prior to its collapse—see video at twf.org/911.html at the beginning, and at 33 seconds.

At the U.S. Department of Energy, where I managed the *U.S. National Power Grid Study* (conducted by 26 teams—150 persons), it would have been highly unusual that a report such as NIST's would be presented to news media without it first being subjected to outside peer review. In fact we had critics review progress of our research at critical stages. NIST has sought to avoid answering its critics. This negates their position.

Except for the photos in the draft report, NIST did not release the photos and videos they referred to at the press briefing for examination by other experts.

The Achilles Heel

Collapse at near free fall speed not explained by government and university investigators

Achilles, the son of King Peleus of Thessaly and the shape-changing nymph Thetis, is the central character of Homer's great poem, the Iliad. The Achilles' heel is named for the only part of the body of the Greek hero that was vulnerable.

Stretching the metaphor a bit, the collapse time, i.e. the time from the initiation of collapse to the total collapse of One and Two World Trade Center, and 7 World Trade Center, is the Achilles' heel of the official 9/11 conspiracy theory.

The official theory is also vulnerable to the challenges outlined in the two previous sections.

The National Institute of Standards and Technology estimates (NIST FAQ, October 5, 2007)

> the elapsed times for the first exterior panels to strike the ground after the collapse initiated in each of the towers to be approximately 11 seconds for WTC 1 and approximately 9 seconds for WTC 2. These elapsed times were based on: (1) precise timing of the ini-

tiation of collapse from video evidence, and
(2) ground motion (seismic) signals recorded
at Palisades, N.Y.

NIST adds:

> significant portions of the cores of both
> buildings (roughly 60 stories of WTC 1
> and 40 stories of WTC 2) are known to
> have stood 15 to 25 seconds after collapse
> initiation before they, too, began to collapse.
> Neither the duration of the seismic records
> nor video evidence . . . are reliable indicators
> of the total time it took for each building to
> collapse completely.

The 9/11 Commission Report simply states (p322):
"the South Tower collapsed in ten seconds".

These collapse times are close to that of a billiard
ball dropped from the top of WTC 1 or 2. The time
is calculated using the equation taught in high school
physics classes:

Distance = 0.5 X Acceleration X Time Squared.

Using this equation a billiard ball dropped from
the top of the 1368 feet tall WTC 1 or 2 would travel
1296 feet in 9 seconds—it would reach the ground in
9.2 seconds (assuming acceleration due to gravity of 32
feet per second per second, and no wind resistance).

The towers' collapse at near free-fall speed, due solely
to airplane impact and the resulting fires, defies logic.

Section 6.14.4 of NIST NCSTAR 1, NIST states:

> the structure below the level of collapse
> initiation offered minimal resistance to
> the falling building mass at and above the

impact zone. The potential energy released by the downward movement of the large building mass far exceeded the capacity of the intact structure below to absorb that energy through energy of deformation.

NIST (a) offers no calculations to support this theory, (b) does not explain the symmetry of collapse, and (c) does not explain how "falling building mass" retains enough energy to destroy the floors below.

The "building mass" has to stay intact in order to cause the structure below it to collapse.

But as we saw on television, the concrete floors of the Twin Towers exploded—into dust, according to many reports—as they came crashing down, and steel beams were hurled outwards.

For the sake of argument only, Prof. Kenneth L. Kuttler assumed One World Trade Center's floors "floating in the air" which did not move till struck from the floors above. Even with this idealized problem, and conservative safety factors in the building's design, Kuttler calculated collapse times of more than 25 seconds due to a gravity only collapse (*Journal of 9/11 Studies*, May 9, 2007).

This result, writes Kuttler "is consistent with the prediction of Gordon Ross in his analysis which concluded that the fall of the North Tower should have been arrested with much of the lower portion of the Tower standing."

Of course, this is not what happened, and no official explanation of the collapse time has been offered.

Flight 93

There is little evidence that Flight 93 ploughed into the ground at the Pennsylvania 'crash site'

Rare television footage from September 11, 2001 contradicts the generally accepted explanation that United Airlines Flight 93 crashed in Shanksville, Pennsylvania at 10:03 a.m., 125 miles from Washington, DC, after four passengers attacked the hijackers in an attempt to gain control of the airplane.

According to *The 9/11 Commission Report*, at 8:42 United Airlines Flight 93 took off from Newark, NJ, bound for San Francisco. It's last "normal contact" with the FAA was at 9:27.

Around 9:28 the Cleveland, OH, controller heard "a radio transmission of unintelligible sounds of possible screaming or a struggle from an unknown origin."

Other transmissions followed, and at 9:30 Ziad Jarrah, the alleged hijacker—a fragment of whose passport was allegedly found at the crash site—(CNN, August 1, 2002), was heard saying,

> There is a bomb on board and are going back to the airport, and to have our demands [unintelligible]. Please remain quiet.

> The FBI believes Jarrah, a Lebanese national, was at the controls of United Airlines Flight 93, . . . U.S. officials believe the plane's target was the White House.

CNN adds that Jarrah "was stopped and questioned in the United Arab Emirates in January 2001 at the request of the CIA, nearly nine months before the attacks".

At 10:01 another aircraft is reported to have witnessed "radical gyrations in what investigators believe was the hijackers' effort to defeat the passenger assault."

However, television footage from September 11, 2001 tells a different story.

> NBC Reporter: "The debris here is spread over a 3 to 4 mile radius which has now been completely sealed off, and is being treated according to the FBI as a crime scene. This is one of those cases where the pictures really do tell the story . . . one of the most horrifying aspects of this is how little debris is visible . . . that's all you see, just a large crater in the ground, and just tiny, tiny bits of debris . . . the investigators out there, and there are hundreds of them, have found nothing larger than a phone book."

A Fox News reporter is heard talking to a Fox affiliate photographer Chris Kanicki [*sic*].

> Fox Reporter: "I've seen the pictures, and it looks like there's nothing there except a hole in the ground."

> Chris : "Basically that is right . . . The only thing you could see was a big gouge in

the earth, and some broken trees . . ."

Fox Reporter: "Any large pieces of debris?"

Chris: "There was nothing that you could distinguish that a plane crashed there . . . nothing going on down there, no smoke, no fire . . .you couldn't see anything, you could see dirt, ash, and people walking around."

Fox Reporter: "How big would you say that hole was?"

Chris: "From my estimate it was 20 to 15 feet long . . . 10 feet wide."

Fox Reporter: "What could you see on the ground other than dirt, ash?"

Chris: "You couldn't see anything . . . just dirt, ash, and people walking around."

Both NBC and Fox reporters make no mention of the Boeing 757's fuselage, tail, landing gear, and engines which would have been found at the "crash site" had the plane plunged to the ground while the "pilot struggled with hijackers."

Elias Davidsson, a researcher in Iceland, reveals anomalies that cast doubt on the authenticity of the transcript from Flight 93's Cockpit Voice Recorder. He writes (*The Events of September 11, 2001 and the Right to the Truth*, April 14, 2008, p16):

The transcripts of CVRs from other crashes around the world . . . mention numerous engine and ambient sounds . . . The transcript of Flight UA 93's CVR does not mention any such sounds and particularly no crash sound at the end . . . the released transcript differed significantly from authentic CVR transcripts by failing to mention the aircraft's ID, the name of the person and agency who issued the transcript and the date the transcript was issued. Furthermore, serious discrepancies have been revealed between what family members heard when the transcript was first played to them by the FBI on April 2, 2002, and what the 9/11 Commission reported to have heard.

Popular accounts of Flight 93 mention several phone calls describing the passengers' struggle with the hijackers, but this is contradicted by the FBI.

According to an FBI report presented as evidence in the trial of Zacarias Moussaoui in 2006, Griffin writes (*Canadian*, October 8, 2007):

there were only two cell phone calls from United 93, and they were made at 9:58, shortly before the plane crashed, when it was down to 5,000 feet. . . . (These two low-altitude calls from Flight 93 were, according to the FBI report, the only two cell phone calls made from all four flights).

Defense Secretary Donald Rumsfeld, during a Christmas Eve address to U.S. troops in Baghdad, said "the people who attacked the United States in New York, shot down the plane over Pennsylvania."

The Pentagon says Rumsfeld "simply misspoke."

There's also the statement by Lee Hamilton, Vice

Chairman of the 9/11 Commission.

While questioning Norman Y. Mineta, Former Secretary of Transportation, Mr. Hamilton asked Mineta about an "order given, I think by the President, that authorized the shooting down of commercial aircraft that were suspected to be controlled by terrorists."

The video of Mineta's testimony before the 9/11 Commission has been removed from the archives of the National Commission on Terrorist Attacks Upon the United States—a copy may be found at The Wisdom Fund's website (twf.org).

Vice President Cheney admitted to giving the order to shoot down hijacked aircraft.

Philip Shenon, an investigative reporter at the New York Times where he has worked since 1981, in *The Commission: The Uncensored History of the 9/11 Investigation* (Twelve, 2008, p264), narrates this exchange between Cheney and Tim Russert (*Meet the Press*, April 4, 2004):

> Russert asked Cheney what was the most difficult decision made during the course of the day [September 11, 2001].
>
> "Well, I suppose the toughest decision was this question of whether or not we would intercept incoming commercial aircraft," Cheney said, referring to the decision to order military jets to shoot down passenger planes that approached Washington.
>
> Russert asked: "And you decided . . ."
>
> Cheney corrected Russert. "We decided to do it." He was referring to himself and

President Bush.

"So if the United States government became aware that a hijacked commercial airliner was destined for the White House or the Capitol, we would take the plane down?" Russert continued.

"Yes," Cheney said somberly.

There is yet another twist to the saga of Flight 93. ABC affiliate WCPO in reported:

A Boeing 767 out of Boston made an emergency landing Tuesday at Cleveland Hopkins International Airport due to concerns that it may have a bomb aboard, said Mayor Michael R. White. . . . United identified the plane as Flight 93.

However, in February 2006, Liz Foreman, whose name was attached to the original story, stated that

an Associated Press bulletin, was posted on WCPO.com during the morning of September 11, 2001. The story stated that Flight 93 landed in Cleveland. This was not true. Once the AP issued a retraction a few minutes later, we removed the link.

On April 28, 2009, Pilots for 9/11 Truth reported that Air Traffic Control radar shows Flight 93 airborne after its reported crash.

The Pentagon

American Airlines, Flight 77, Boeing 757 were not mentioned at the Pentagon News Briefing

The evidence shows that American Airlines Flight 77 did not strike the Pentagon on September 11, 2001—the laws of science refute the official account of 9/11

At the September 12, 2001, Dept. of Defense News Briefing, American Airlines, Flight 77, Boeing 757 were not even mentioned.

The security camera video of "Flight 77" released by the Pentagon has one frame showing something— labeled "Approaching Aircraft"—moving parallel to the ground about 100 yards in front of the Pentagon.

That's the U.S. government's evidence to support its claim that American Airlines Flight 77 struck the Pentagon on September 11, 2001.

However, the government's own records — Pentagon transcripts, official reports, flight data recorder, and the laws of science belie *The 9/11 Commission Report.*

Eyewitness Accounts

Just minutes after the alleged attack, standing in front of the Pentagon on September 11, 2001, Jamie McIntyre, CNN's senior Pentagon correspondent since

November 1992, reported:

> From my close up inspection there's no evidence of a plane having crashed anywhere near the Pentagon. . . . The only pieces left that you can see are small enough that you could pick up in your hand. There are no large tail sections, wing sections, fuselage — nothing like that anywhere around which would indicate that the entire plane crashed into the side of the Pentagon.

McIntyre continued,

> If you look at the pictures of the Pentagon you see that all of the floors have collapsed, that didn't happen immediately. It wasn't till almost 45 minutes later that the structure was weakened enough that all of the floors collapsed.

This news report apparently was not rebroadcast, and a few years later McIntyre claimed on CNN (Wolf Blitzer's show) that he had been taken out of context.

Jamie McIntyre's account is confirmed by Lt Robert Medairos, Arlington County Police—incident commander on September 11, who stated (ABC 7 at 3:25 p.m.), "They said it was a plane, and I didn't see any pieces of any plane, and I couldn't believe a plane hit the building."

Lt Col Karen Kwiatowski, who from her fifth-floor, B Ring office at the Pentagon, witnessed "an unforgettable fireball, 20 to 30 feet in diameter" confirms McIntyre's account.

Writing in *9/11 and American Empire: Intellectuals*

Speak Out, Kwiatowski noted,

> a strange absence of airliner debris, there
> was no sign of the kind of damage to the
> Pentagon structure one would expect from
> the impact of a large airliner. This visible
> evidence or lack thereof may also have been
> apparent to the secretary of defense, who in
> an unfortunate slip of the tongue referred to
> the aircraft that slammed into the Pentagon
> as a 'missile'.

Pentagon employee April Gallop, whose "desk was roughly 40 feet from the point where the plane allegedly hit the outside wall" stated in a sworn complaint (before the U.S. District Court Southern District of New York):

> As she sat down to work there was an explo-
> sion, then another; walls collapsed and the
> ceiling fell in. Hit in the head, she was able
> to grab the baby and make her way towards
> the daylight showing through a blasted
> opening in the outside wall. There was no
> airplane wreckage and no burning airplane
> fuel anywhere; only rubble and dust.

Barbara Honegger, military affairs journalist, re-ported in her personal capacity that a pilot sent by Gen Larry Arnold (NORAD) "reported back that there was no evidence that a plane had hit the building."

Honegger adds, "Multiple standard-issue, battery-operated wall clocks . . . stopped between 9:31 and 9:32-1/2 on September 11"—a few minutes before Flight 77 is alleged to have struck the Pentagon at 9:38.

Major General Albert Stubblebine, U.S. Army (ret)

—former Commanding General of U.S. Army Intelligence and Security Command, and head of Imagery
Interpretation for Scientific and Technical Intelligence
—stated in a video interview,

> I don't know exactly what hit it, but I do
> know, from the photographs that I have
> analyzed and looked at very, very carefully,
> it was not an airplane.

Major Douglas Rokke, U.S. Army (ret) adds:

> No aircraft hit the Pentagon. Totally impos-
> sible! You couldn't make the turns with a
> 757. You couldn't fly it in over the highway.
> You couldn't fly it over the light poles. You
> couldn't even get it that close to the ground
> because of turbulence.

Other eyewitnesses, however, did report seeing a
plane hit the Pentagon. The evidence does not support
their accounts.

Phone Calls From Flight 77

In a front page article on September 12, 2001—On
Flight 77: 'Our Plane Is Being Hijacked'—Marc Fisher
and Don Phillips of the *Washington Post* reported that
Barbara K. Olson called her husband twice in the final
minutes before the crash of Flight 77. The FBI contradicts this account.

According to the *Washington Post*, Olson's last words
to her husband were, "What do I tell the pilot to do?"

"She called from the plane while it was being hijacked," said Theodore Olson—42nd Solicitor General
of the United States. "I wish it wasn't so, but it is."

"The two conversations each lasted about a minute,

said Tim O'Brien, a CNN reporter and friend of the Olsons."

However, FBI exhibit (P200054 above) from the trial of Zacarias Moussaoui contradicts the Solicitor General's account. It shows that Barbara Olson made only one phone call—it did not connect, and it lasted for 0 seconds.

September 12, 2001: Pentagon News Briefing

At the September 12, 2001, Dept. of Defense (DoD) News Briefing by Assistant Secretary of Defense, Victoria Clarke, Ed Plaugher (fire chief of Arlington County), and others—with the world's news media assembled— "American Airlines", "Flight 77", "Boeing 757" were not even mentioned.

Fire chief Ed Plaugher when asked by a reporter, "Is there anything left of the aircraft at all?" responded, "there are some small pieces of aircraft . . . there's no fuselage sections and that sort of thing."

When asked, "Chief, there are small pieces of the plane virtually all over, out over the highway, tiny pieces. Would you say the plane exploded, virtually exploded on impact due to the fuel", Plaugher reponded "You know, I'd rather not comment on that."

The transcript reveals that reporters were being "threatened or, in fact, handcuffed and dragged away".

September 15, 2001: Pentagon News Briefing

At the September 15, 2001, Dept. of Defense (DoD) News Briefing by Mr. Lee Evey, Pentagon Renovation Manager, Rear Adm. Craig R. Quigley, deputy assistant secretary of Defense for Public Affairs, and others, it was apparent that there were lingering doubts about what had struck the Pentagon on September 11.

When Mr. Evey said, "the nose of the aircraft broke through this innermost wall of C Ring", a reporter asked,

> One thing that's confusing—if it came in the way you described, at an angle, why then are not the wings outside? I mean, the wings would have shorn off. The tail would have shorn off. And yet there's apparently no evidence of the aircraft outside the E Ring.

Apparently, no one asked how "the nose of the aircraft" (a relatively weak component of the aircraft) remained sufficiently intact to penetrate the C Ring.

Pentagon Building Performance Report

In January 2003, the U.S. government's National Institute of Standards and Technology released the *Pentagon Building Performance Report.*

Page 35 of this report reads:

> An examination of the area encompassed by extending the line of travel of the aircraft to the face of the building shows that there are no discrete marks on the building corresponding to the positions of the outer third of the right wing. The size and position of the actual opening in the facade of the building (from column line 8 to column line 18) indicate that no portion of the outer two-thirds of the right wing and no portion of the outer one-third of the left wing actually entered the building.

The wings of a Boeing 757 were not found outside

the Pentagon. Photographs, and CNN's Jamie McIntyre confirm this fact.

Page 36 of the *Pentagon Building Performance Report* reads:

> The height of the damage to the facade of the building was much less than the height of the aircraft's tail. At approximately 45 ft, the tail height was nearly as tall as the first four floors of the building. Obvious visible damage extended only over the lowest two floors, to approximately 25 ft above grade.

This implies that whatever struck the Pentagon, couldn't have been a Boeing 757.

Page 39 of the *Pentagon Building Performance Report* reads:

> Most likely, the wings of the aircraft were severed as the aircraft penetrated the facade of the building. Even if portions of the wings remained intact after passing through the plane of the facade, the structural damage pattern indicates that the wings were severed before the aircraft penetrated more than a few dozen feet into the building.

The *Pentagon Building Performance Report* (Figure 7.9) indicates a "Slab deflected upward" which is consistent with either an explosion below the slab, or an upward blow by a hard object.

From the preceding it is clear that the *Pentagon Building Performance Report*—prepared by the American Society of Civil Engineers and the Structural Engineering Institute, and released by the U.S. government's

National Institute of Standards and Technology —contradicts the official account of 9/11.

Arlington County After-Action Report

The *Arlington County After-Action Report* describes the occurrence of an event at the Pentagon minutes before the alleged strike of Flight 77, and the presence of Fort Myer Unit 161 at the Pentagon prior to impact.

Annex A, Page A-4 of the *Arlington County After-Action Report* report states:

> Captain Dennis Gilroy and his team were already on station at the Pentagon when Flight #77 slammed into it, just beyond the heliport. Foam 161 caught fire and suffered a flat tire from flying debris. Firefighters Mark Skipper and Alan Wallace were outside the vehicle at impact and received burns and lacerations. . . . Captain Gilroy called the Fort Myer Fire Department, reporting for the first time the actual location of the crash.

Fort Myer Unit 161 arrival at the Pentagon prior to the alleged strike by Flight 77 is consistent with a reporter's question at the September 12 News Briefing,

> Chief, there are small pieces of the plane virtually all over, out over the highway, tiny pieces. Would you say the plane exploded, virtually exploded on impact due to the fuel?

It is consistent with April Gallop's sworn complaint she was able to grab the baby and make her way towards the daylight showing through a blasted opening in the outside wall. There was no airplane wreckage and no burning airplane fuel anywhere; only rubble and dust.

It is consistent with military affairs journalist Barbara Honegger's account of "Multiple standard-issue, battery-operated wall clocks . . . stopped between 9:31 and 9:32-1/2 on September 11."

The report's Appendix 1, 24-Hour Timeline, does not mention Fort Myer Unit 161's presence at the Pentagon prior to the strike by "Flight 77".

The 24-Hour Timeline, also does not mention Arlington County Fire Department Engine 102 and Engine 107 clearly seen in photos at the Pentagon on September 11, 2001.

'American Airlines' Flight Data Recorder

Pilots for 9/11 Truth state: "video captured by the parking gate cam is in direct conflict with the Aircraft Flight Data Recorder data released by the NTSB"—the National Transportation Safety Board, pursuant to a Freedom of Information Act request. *The Pentagon Building Performance Report* states (p14):

> A Pentagon security camera located near the northwest corner of the building recorded the aircraft as it approached the building. Five photographs (figures 3.3 through 3.7), taken approximately one second apart, show the approaching aircraft and the ensuing fireball associated with the initial impact."

On page 35 of this report we're told,

> The site data indicate that the aircraft fuselage impacted the building at column line 14 at an angle of approximately 42 degrees

to the normal to the face of the building, at
or slightly below the second-story slab.

However, the NTSB animation (January 2002), according to Pilots for 9/11 Truth, shows an aircraft flying north of the Navy Annex, not leveling off, and being too high to have hit the Pentagon.

When confronted with this discrepancy, NTSB Chief Jim Potter said: "I have no comment on the existence of the discrepancies."

Two Pentagon security officers state categorically that a plane (which they believed was Flight 77) flew north of the Citgo gas station (now demolished) located west of the Pentagon on South Joyce Street at Columbia Pike, rather than flying south of the gas station as stated in official reports.

Damage Not Consistent With Boeing 757 Strike

With Flight 77 alleged to have struck the Pentagon at "an angle of approximately 42 degrees", the flight path and damage path are unlikely to form a straight line.

Flying at "an angle of approximately 42 degrees" the Boeing 757's starboard wing would have struck the west wall of the Pentagon before the port wing. This would cause the aircraft to veer to the right, and the damage path would be in line with the aircraft's new heading—not with the aircraft's heading prior to impact (assuming, miraculously, the plane was able to penetrate the C Ring—the outermost is E Ring).

However, the *Pentagon Building Performance Report* Figures 6.2 and 6.6 show that the flight path and damage path (damage path also illustrated in the *Arlington*

County After Action Report, p23) do form a straight line extending from the center-line of the fuselage of the aircraft to where the "the nose of the aircraft broke through this innermost wall of C Ring".

If the wings had sheared off, they would have been seen by Plaugher and Medairos. If the wings had sliced through, we would have a 125 ft opening—the wingspan of a Boeing 75—in the outer wall. Neither occurred.

Also, observed damage did not extend to the height of the aircraft's tail.

G-Force Would Have Destroyed the Boeing 757

Pilots for 9/11 Truth conclude: "Arlington's unique topography and obstacles along American 77 'final leg' to the Pentagon make this approach completely impossible".

Flight 77 is alleged to have flown over Columbia Pike and the Virginia Department of Transportation communications tower located 1143 yards west of the Pentagon before striking the Pentagon at "530 miles per hour".

The antenna on the VDOT tower has been determined to be 169 ft above the ground with a ground elevation of 135 feet (FCC Registration Number 1016111). The ground elevation of the Pentagon is 33 feet according to USGS.

This path would have taken Flight 77 south of the Citgo gas station (now demolished) at the intersection of Columbia Pike and S. Joyce Street, and over the intersection of Columbia Pike and Virginia Route 27.

Flight 77 would then have been over Pentagon

grounds with about 500 feet remaining to level out and to strike the Pentagon "slightly below the second floor slab" at "an angle of approximately 42 degrees".

The Columbia Pike and VA-27 intersection presents a roughly 20 feet tall barrier in the alleged path of Flight 77.

According to the *Pentagon Building Performance Report* (p14),

> The first photograph (figure 3.3) captured an image of the aircraft when it was approximately 320 ft (approximately 0.42 second) from impact with the west wall of the Pentagon. Two photographs (figures 3.3 and 3.7), when compared, seem to show that the top of the fuselage of the aircraft was no more than approximately 20 ft above the ground when the first photograph of this series was taken.

Leaving aside the discrepancies between the official account of Flight 77, and the Flight Data Recorder (which NTSB refuses to answer), Pilots for 9/11 Truth calculated the force on the Boeing 757 at 34 Gs, i.e. 34 times the force due to gravity, at the point that it would have to transition from its downward flight to level flight.

With a virtual weight of about 8.5 million pounds, Flight 77 could not have leveled off before striking the Pentagon. This alone is sufficient to refute the official account of "Flight 77"—Flight 77 cannot have violated the laws of science.

Pilots for 9/11 Truth did another calculation by lowering the height of "Flight 77" below that shown by the

FDR. They lowered it to the top of the VDOT antenna beside Columbia Pike — under the alleged flight path.

With this very conservative case, they calculated the force on the Boeing 757 at 11.2 Gs. "11.2 Gs was never recorded in the FDR. 11.2 Gs would rip the aircraft apart" they wrote.

Conclusion

The official account of Flight 77—supported only by one frame from a security camera showing a puff of something approaching the Pentagon—is contradicted by eyewitnesses, by the transcripts of Pentagon News Briefings conducted on September 12 and 15, by the *Pentagon Building Performance Report*, by the *Arlington County After-Action Report*, by the FBI's exhibit on phone calls from Flight 77, and by the Flight Data Recorder provided by the NTSB.

The official account of Flight 77 contradicts the laws of science. Flight 77 could not have withstood the calculated G-force when it would have had to level out at "530 miles per hour"—about 100 yards before striking the Pentagon— with "the top of the fuselage of the aircraft . . . no more than approximately 20 ft above the ground".

On September 10, 2001, then Secretary of Defense Donald Rumsfeld admitted that the Pentagon "cannot track $2.3 trillion in transactions". It is alleged that the section of the Pentagon destroyed on September 11, 2001 housed records of DoD spending.

Boomerang

By March 2003, with the Commission's staff barely in place, a detailed outline, complete with "chapter headings, subheadings, and sub-subheadings" of *The 9/11 Commission Report* had been prepared (Shenon, p389). At the first public hearing, Chairman Kean asked, "What kind of fanaticism drove them to do this?"

With the goal set, contradictory evidence was excluded; the final report was fatally flawed.

Bin Laden is not wanted by the FBI for 9/11.

There were no Arab names on the published passenger lists, several of the hijackers are reported to be alive, the 9/11 Commission ignored the discrepancies.

Aircraft impact and the resulting fires could not have brought down the Twin Towers—evidence of explosives was ignored by the 9/11 Commission.

The collapse of the 47-story 7 World Trade Center in about seven seconds has yet to be explained —NIST's computer simulation is inconclusive.

There's little or no evidence that Flight 93 ploughed into the ground at the Pennsylvania "crash site".

There's no hard evidence that Flight 77 struck the Pentagon—photos, videos, and other evidence is being withheld by the U.S. government.

The architects of the 9/11 attacks have yet to be unveiled. To begin to identify them one needs to answer: Who is responsible for the continuing cover-up? Who had the motive, means, and opportunity to carry out these attacks? Who benefited?

But the U.S. government is anxious to avoid having *The 9/11 Commission Report* scrutinized too closely, and is not interested in an independent investigation.

According to Sahr MuhammedAlly, who observed part of the proceedings at Guantanamo, during the war crimes tribunal—the first since WWII—convened to try Bin Laden's onetime driver, Salim Hamdan, the government claimed that *The 9/11 Commssion Report*—a *New York Times* bestseller—was classified and could not be used in the trial (democracynow.org, August 7, 2008)!

The credibility of the Bush administration, and America's reputation, are at an all-time low. The dollar has plunged, the U.S. economy is in recession, and taxpayers are stuck with about a trillion dollar bill to bailout failing banks. The "peace dividend" has been squandered.

> In 1989, *The Washington Post* reported that
>> military experts from previous administrations told Congress today that the $300 billion annual Pentagon budget could be safely cut in half over the next decade because of the reduced threat from the Soviet Union and Eastern Europe.

The war on "war on terrorism" has boomeranged.

Nobel Prize-winning economist Joseph Stiglitz, and Harvard economist Linda Bilmes, estimate the cost of the Iraq war at $3 to $5 trillion. At a time when funds are needed for health care, education, infrastructure, that's $10,000 to over $16,000 for every American.

This is in addition to the $481 billion budgeted for defense in 2008. Compare this to $500 billion budgeted by the rest of the world combined!

It is reported that more than 4000 American soldiers have died, 320,000 had brain injuries, and 300,000 U.S. veterans have mental problem (Pauline Jelinek, Associated Press, April 17, 2008).

The United Nations Compensation Commission imposed a total of $53 billion in war reparations charges against Iraq for its invasion of Kuwait in 1990. What does the U.S. owe Iraq in reparations?

In the 10 years prior to the U.S. invasion of Iraq, 500,000 children and old people died as a result of U.S.-UN sanctions. More than 1.1 million have died as a result of the invasion (Fairness & Accuracy in Reporting, January/February 2008):

> [A] Johns Hopkins study estimated that, as of July 2006, 655,000 Iraqis had been killed, about 600,000 of them violently and at least 30 percent directly by coalition forces. It updated an earlier study (Lancet, 10/29/04) that estimated that 100,000 Iraqis had died during the first year of the war. An extrapolation of the Johns Hopkins estimate of violent deaths done by Just Foreign Policy (9/18/07) currently stands at over 1.1 million.

In the U.S., "North Korea and Iran are seen as the

biggest risks. However, the youngest U.S. respondents share the Europeans' view that theirs is the biggest threat, with 35 per cent of American 16- to 24-year-olds identifying it [U.S.] as the chief danger to stability", according to a survey by Harris Research for the *Financial Times* (July 1, 2007).

The American Human Development Report (July 16, 2008) funded by Oxfam America, the Conrad Hilton Foundation, and Rockefeller Foundation, found that the U.S. had slumped from 2nd place in 1990 to 12th place.

Following the collapse of the Soviet Union in 1991, the U.S. needed new "enemies" to justify maintaining the bloated military-industrial complex, and to control the resources and markets of other countries which it has done for decades.

U.S. strategists settled on creating the "Islamic fundamentalist" threat (Leon T. Hadar, Cato Institute, August 27, 1992).

"Islamic fundamentalist" evolved, and became the "rogue states and nuclear outlaws," the "axis of evil," the "war on terrorism," and "Islamo-fascism."

General Wesley Clark, former NATO Supreme Allied Commander, during an interview televised on Democracy Now! (March 2, 2007) stated:

> About 10 days after 9/11, I went through the Pentagon, . . . and one of the generals called me in. . . . He says, "We've made the decision we're going to war with Iraq." . . .
>
> So I came back to see him a few weeks later, and by that time we were bombing in Afghanistan. I said, "Are we still going to war

> with Iraq?" And he said, "Oh, it's worse than that." . . . "This is a memo that describes how we're going to take out seven countries in five years, starting with Iraq, and then Syria, Lebanon, Libya, Somalia, Sudan and, finishing off, Iran.

While most Americans seek an end to the Iraq war, "Israel and its Fifth Column in this city seek to stampede us into war with Iran" writes Patrick J. Buchanan —senior adviser to American presidents Richard Nixon, Gerald Ford, and Ronald Reagan.

Meanwhile the killing goes on.

Americans and Muslims are dying in wars promoted by the military, industrial, congressional complex, global corporations, Israel, and Christian Zionists.

Former Supreme Court Justice Robert Jackson, chief U.S. prosecutor at the first Nuremberg trial, has called waging aggressive war "the supreme international crime differing only from other war crimes in that it contains within itself the accumulated evil of the whole" (Benjamin B. Ferencz, Salzburg Law School, Summer 2004).

For the military-industrial complex and global corporations wars are for profit. For Israel, wars are for land, water, and regional supremacy. For Christian Zionists the target is Islam.

In February 24, 1948, George Kennan—one of the most influential figures of the Cold War, stated in the top secret *Policy Planning Study 23* for the U.S. Department of State:

> we have about 50% of the world's wealth but only 6.3 % of its population. . . . Our

real task in the coming period is to devise a pattern of relationships which will permit us to maintain this position of disparity . . .

According to historian R. T. Naylor (Standard Schaeffer, *CounterPunch*, June 21, 2003):

Al-Qaeda itself does not exist, except in the fevered imaginations of neo-cons and Likudniks . . . who find it extremely useful as a bogeyman to spook the public and the politicians to acquiesce in otherwise unacceptable policy initiatives at home and abroad. Very simply, what you have are loose networks of likeminded individuals . . . They conduct their operations strictly by themselves, even if they may from time to time seek advice.

In *Who Speaks for Islam?*, a product of the Gallup World Poll's massive research, authors John L. Esposito and Dalia Mogahed find that Muslims around the world want basically what Americans want. They reject terrorism, they admire the West for its technology and democracy. What they least admire about the West is its perceived moral decay and breakdown of traditional values. They criticize or celebrate countries based on their politics, not based on their culture or religion.

The "clash of civilizations" exists only in the imaginations of those who lead us to war for money or power. Ultimately, most wars are a clash of values—greed versus justice.

❖

Muslims Didn't Do It

"All the proffered evidence that America was attacked by Muslims on 9/11, when subjected to critical scrutiny, appears to have been fabricated."—David Ray Griffin, Professor Emeritus

Military and Intelligence Professionals

"I'm astounded that the conspiracy theory advanced by the administration could in fact be true and the evidence does not seem to suggest that that's accurate."—Col. Ronald D. Ray, U.S. Marine Corps (ret)

"Scholars and professionals . . . have established beyond any reasonable doubt that the official account of 9/11 is false and that, therefore, the official 'investigations' have really been cover-up operations."—Lt. Col. Robert Bowman, PhD, U.S. Air Force (ret)

"Your countrymen have been murdered and the more you delve into it the more it looks as though they were murdered by our government, who used it as an excuse to murder other people thousands of miles away."—Lt. Col. Shelton F. Lankford, U.S. Marine Corps (ret)

"It is as a scientist that I have the most trouble with the official government conspiracy theory, mainly because it does not satisfy the rules of probability or physics."—Lt. Col. Karen U. Kwiatkowski, PhD, U.S. Air Force (ret)

"No aircraft hit the Pentagon. Totally impossible! You couldn't make the turns with a 757. You couldn't fly it in over the highway. You couldn't fly it over the light poles. You couldn't even get it that close to the ground because of turbulence."—Major Douglas Rokke, PhD, U.S. Army (ret)

"The government story they handed us about 9/11 is total B.S. plain and simple."—Capt. Russ Wittenberg, U.S. Air Force

"[W]hat we saw happen on that morning of September 11, 2001, was the result of a highly-compartmentalized covert operation to bring about a fascist coup in this country."—Alan N. Sabrosky, PhD

Pilots and Aviation Professionals

"We analyzed the data and announced our conclusion on 3/26/07 that 'The information provided by the NTSB does not support the 9/11 Commission Report of American Airlines Flight 77 impact with the Pentagon.'"—Rob Balsamo, Commercial airline pilot, Co-founder Pilots for 9/11 Truth

"I most certainly and honestly believe, that sometime in the near future, it will become common knowledge that the events of 9/11 were an 'inside job' designed, engineered and committed by a very large and 'in control' rogue element within our United States federal government".—Glen Stanish, Commercial airline pilot

"No Boeing 757 ever crashed into the Pentagon. No Boeing 757 ever crashed at Shanksville. . . . And no Arab hijacker, ever in a million years, ever flew into the World Trade Center. And if you got 30 minutes I'll tell you exactly why he couldn't do it the first time."—John Lear, Retired commercial airline pilot

". . . an airplane that weighs 100 tons all assembled is still going to have 100 tons of disassembled trash and parts after it hits a building. There was no wreckage from a 757 at the Pentagon."—Capt. Russ Wittenberg, Retired commercial pilot

"I was also a Navy fighter pilot and Air Combat Instructor, U.S. Navy Fighter Weapons School and have experience flying low altitude, high speed aircraft. I could not have done what these beginners did."—Commander Ralph Kolstad, Retired commercial airline captain

"I know from my experience that it would have been highly improbable that even a seasoned American test pilot, a military test pilot, could have flown a T-category, aircraft like the 757, into the first floor of the Pentagon because of a thing called Ground Effect."—Capt. Fred Fox, Retired commercial airline pilot

"The Pentagon was not hit by a Boeing 757. A Boeing 757 did not crash in Shanksville Pa."—Gordon Price, Retired commercial airline captain

Engineers and Architects

"The 9/11 Commission Report is fatally flawed. The major conclusions of the 9/11 Commission Report (the official, conspiracy theory) are false."—Enver Masud, Engineer and author "9/11 Unveiled"

"I will present to you the very clear evidence that all three World Trade Center high-rise buildings, the Twin Towers and Building 7 were destroyed not by fire as our government has told us, but by controlled demolition with explosives."—Richard Gage, Founding member of Architects and Engineers for 9/11 Truth

"I have 'known' from day-one that the buildings were imploded and that they could not and would not have collapsed from the damage caused by the airplanes that ran into them."—Daniel B. Barnum, B.Arch, FAIA

"[S]ymmetrical collapse is strong evidence of a controlled demolition. A building falling from asymmetrical structural failure would not collapse so neatly, nor so rapidly".—David A. Johnson, B.Arch, MCP, PhD, F.AICP

"Obviously it [WTC 7] was the result of controlled demolition and scheduled to take place during the confusion surrounding the day's events."—Jack Keller, BS CE, MS Irrigation Eng, PhD Agricultural and Irrigation Eng, PE, F.ASCE

"In my opinion the building WTC 7 was, with great probability, professionally demolished".—Hugo Bachmann, PhD

"The [Twin Tower] building was designed to have a fully loaded 707 crash into it. That was the largest plane at the time. I believe that the building probably could sustain multiple impacts of jetliners because this structure is like the mosquito netting on your screen door."—Frank A. DeMartini, Architect and WTC Construction Manager

"I looked at the drawings, the construction and it couldn't be done by fire. So, no, absolutely not."—Danny Jowenko, Proprietor, Jowenko Explosieve Demolitie B.V.

Professors

"We have found solid scientific grounds on which to question the interpretation put upon the events of September 11, 2001 by the Office of the President of the United States of America and subsequently propagated by the major media of western nations."—A. K. Dewdney, PhD, Member Scientific Panel Investigating Nine-Eleven

"Despite the absence of any visible fire at the time of collapse, the government report alleges WTC Building 7 is the first and only steel-framed high-rise building in the history of mankind to collapse simply as the result of a fire."—David L. Griscom, Research physicist, Member Scholars for 9/11 Truth and Justice

"Truth, Ethics and Professionalism are completely lacking in the official aftermath and investigations surrounding the 911 disasters. Unfortunately we went to war predicated on lies, sustained in lies, and perpetuated in lies."—Hamid Mumin, Ph.D., P.Eng., P.Geo.

"In my opinion the building WTC 7 was, with great probability, professionally demolished".—Jorg Schneider, Dr hc, Professor Emeritus, Structural Dynamics and Earthquake Engineering

"This is the first time, and this is the worst disaster, but this is the first time that families have been attempted to be silenced through a special fund, . . . I found that the airlines approached members of Congress and the Senate to get their bailout and their immunity and their protection starting on 9/11."—Mary Schiavo, JD, Former Professor of Aviation

"On the basis of photographic and video evidence as well as related data and analyses, I provide thirteen reasons for rejecting the official hypothesis, according to which fire and impact damage caused the collapse of the Twin Towers and WTC 7, in favor of the controlled-demolition hypothesis."—Steven Jones, PhD, Former Professor of Physics

Praise for *The War on Islam* by Enver Masud

"Enver Masud gives example after example of disinformation and lies, cover-ups and double standards."—*Impact International*, England

"He brings balanced analysis of world affairs amidst the chaos of doctored evidence and complacent media."—*Muslim Observer*, USA

"Excellent tool for explaining the realities of the world."—Muslimedia International, Canada

"The contents of the book are an eye opener."—All India Conference of Intellectuals, India

"One thing that is particularly impressive about the articles is Masud's obvious depth of knowledge about the U.S. and its policies in the world, and the way he is able to bring in impressive and telling statistics and background information to support his arguments and his case."—*Crescent International*, Canada

"Of historical significance, . . . A book like this is desperately needed in the warmongering climate of today."—*Muslims*, New York

"Excellent book. Dispels the myths and commonly held misconceptions about Islam."—Human Rights Foundation, South Africa

"A masterpiece of information of present day happenings in the world."—Tasmia Educational and Social Welfare Society, India

"His thoughts may prove valuable to thinking people in America"—Mumia Abu Jamal, USA

"One of the few contemporary voices of reason and wisdom"—William Mark Hardiker (freelance journalist), Australia

250,000+ sold or downloaded

The Human Rights Foundation of South Africa
hereby acknowledges the contributions of
Mr. Enver Masud, author of *The War on Islam*
for his efforts in dedicating himself to unveiling
the truth regarding the onslaught against Islam.
His book is a superb contribution to the truth.
This gold award is granted to
Mr. Enver Masud
on 17 April 2002
South Africa

❖

American Federation of Muslims
of Indian Origin (AFMI)
2003 Award of Excellence
Presented to
Enver Masud
For his outstanding achievements
and for his distinguished services
in promoting greater understanding
of Islam and Muslims
September 27, 2003

❖

United States Department of Energy
Cash Award for Superior Job Performance
Presented to
Enver Masud
In recognition of the high quality of his professionalism,
his perseverance, and his competence . . .
June 1980

9/11 Unveiled presented to:

Thomas H. Kean, Chair
The 9/11 Commission
June 23, 2011

President Barack H. Obama
August 15, 2012

International Criminal Court
October 1, 2012